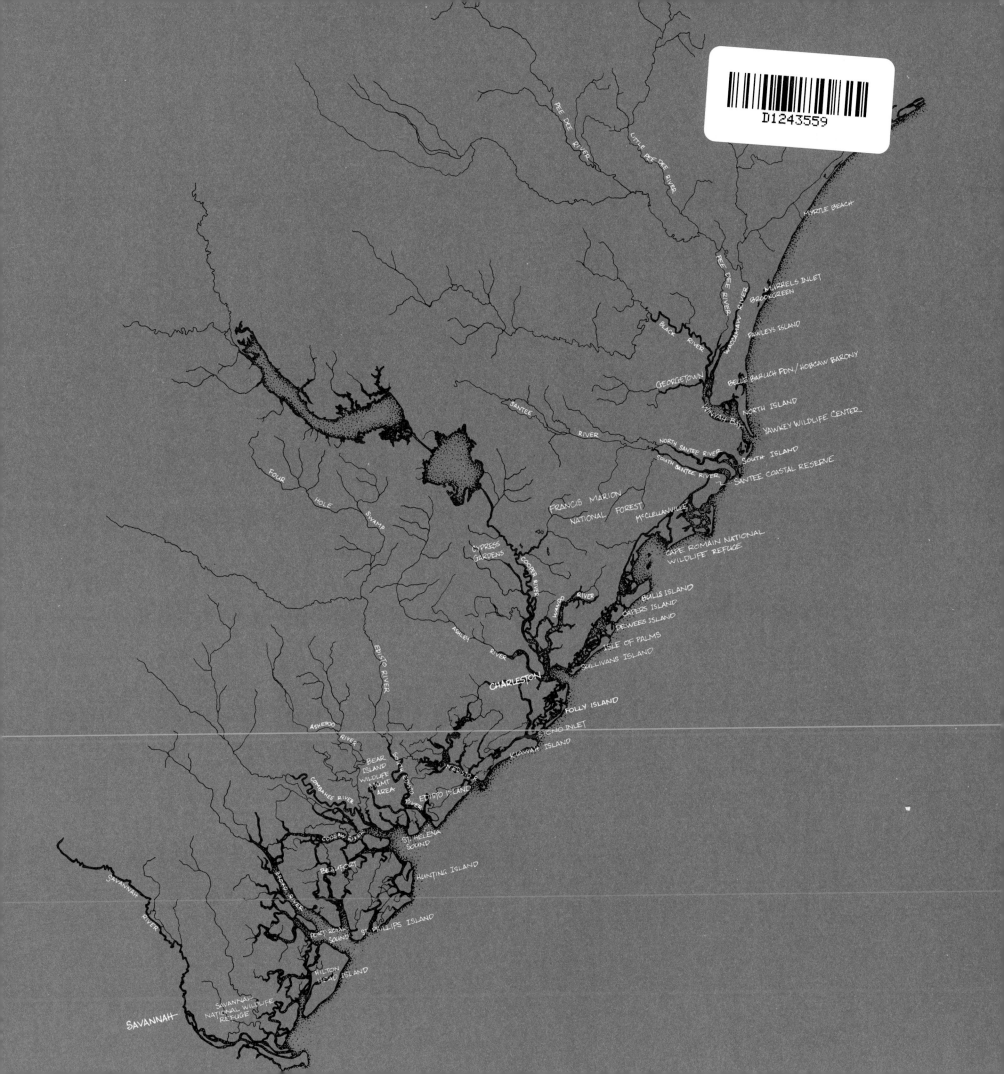

PEE DEE RIVER

LITTLE PEE DEE RIVER

MYRTLE BEACH

PEE DEE RIVER

WACCAMAW RIVER

MURRELS INLET

BROOKGREEN

BLACK RIVER

PAWLEYS ISLAND

BELLE BARUCH FDN./HOBCAW BARONY

GEORGETOWN

SANTEE

NORTH ISLAND

WINYAH BAY

YAWKEY WILDLIFE CENTER

RIVER

NORTH SANTEE RIVER

SOUTH SANTEE RIVER

SOUTH ISLAND

SANTEE COASTAL RESERVE

FOUR

FRANCIS MARION

NATIONAL FOREST

McCLELLANVILLE

HOLE

SWAMP

CYPRESS GARDENS

COOPER RIVER

CAPE ROMAIN NATIONAL WILDLIFE REFUGE

BULLS ISLAND

WANDO RIVER

CAPERS ISLAND

DEWEES ISLAND

ASHLEY RIVER

ISLE OF PALMS

SULLIVANS ISLAND

EDISTO RIVER

CHARLESTON

FOLLY ISLAND

ASHEPOO RIVER

STONO INLET

KIAWAH ISLAND

BEAR ISLAND WILDLIFE MGMT AREA

COMBAHEE RIVER

N EDISTO

S EDISTO

EDISTO ISLAND

COOSAW RIVER

ST. HELENA SOUND

SAVANNAH RIVER

BEAUFORT

HUNTING ISLAND

BROAD RIVER

PORT ROYAL SOUND

ST PHILLIPS ISLAND

HILTON HEAD ISLAND

SAVANNAH

SAVANNAH NATIONAL WILDLIFE REFUGE

Dawn on the Santee River Delta

Live oak, Spanish moss and marsh, Edisto Island

LOWCOUNTRY
The Natural Landscape

Photographs by

Tom Blagden, Jr.

Text by

Jane Lareau & Richard Porcher

Legacy Publications

A Subsidiary of Pace Communications
Greensboro, North Carolina

For my parents,

Tom and Martha Blagden,

who taught me to

"Rise free from care before the dawn,
  and seek adventures.
  Let the noon find thee by other lakes,
  and the night overtake thee everywhere at home."

                    Henry David Thoreau
                    Walden

Text Copyright © 1988 Jane Lareau
Photographs, "Introduction," "Comments on Photography,"
Copyright © 1988 Tom Blagden, Jr.

Designed by Lee Helmer
Edited by D. J. Bost

Library of Congress Catalog Card Number: 88-81582

ISBN 0-933101-12-0

Printed in Hong Kong by Everbest Printing Company
through Four Colour Imports Ltd., Louisville, Kentucky.

CONTENTS

Southern wild rice, Cuckolds Creek, Combahee River

INTRODUCTION

To see the Lowcountry is to perceive its light — the light which defines a spacious, horizontal landscape. The weather determines its moods and gives life to the land. The geography is loose, bounded by soft edges and ill-defined by the migrations of water, wind, and sand. It is a realm of interwoven textures, patterns and colors where the intense brightness of open expanses contrasts with the shadowed world of forest and swamp. There is little of hard structure — no granite cliffs or rocky riverbeds. No monumental forms. Instead, the Lowcountry is a world of malleable substances teaming with life, constantly changing.

The Lowcountry defies exact geographic location. It extends roughly from the Waccamaw River plantations in South Carolina to Savannah, Georgia—a watery maze of rivers, swamps, forests, marshes, and barrier islands; a coastal strip where the ocean is forever dominant. The land is inherently low-lying, and as the sea floods and ebbs, so do the riverine currents that flow into it, with tidal shifts reaching far inland.

Here also is a place of contradictions where meandering rivers, milky light and endless marsh seem so benign, yet where the heat, insects and steamy jungle can be most inhospitable. Yet the Lowcountry embodies a spirit that is palpable, a spirit unique to the coast of South Carolina. The elements of earth, air and water are fused in intricate energy webs, creating a region that is soft and lush, a sense of place that is both wild and subtle.

It is easy to take for granted this Lowcountry wildness. More than 40 percent of the South Carolina coast is protected in preserves and refuges, and the state holds one quarter of the remaining tidal marshlands on the entire Atlantic seaboard. In addition to federal, state, and trust reserves, numerous private plantations from the rice culture era devote hundreds of thousands of acres to wildlife habitat and land preservation.

It is ironic, however, that the photographs in this book evoke the illusion of wilderness, for "wilderness" it is not. Virtually all of the South Carolina coast has been altered at one time or another during the course of 300 years of settlement. The Lowcountry is a transformed and transitional landscape, not only by natural forces but more radically by the dreams and demands of man. The ensuing text by Jane Lareau and Richard Porcher portrays the natural landscape of the Lowcountry in a historic context, reflecting our cultural values and allowing us to perceive how this land evolved and perhaps where it is going.

The photographs are about the emotional essence of the Lowcountry. I did not strive to understand or document it, but rather to convey the experience of being immersed in it. These images are personal and symbolic, representing years of discovery, only to find that the more I look, the more there is still to see. Such is the Lowcountry — a land we seek to know, for it entices us with its hypnotic motion of water and wind. Its elusive state of flux keeps us exploring its metamorphic nature. We can love the Lowcountry, in part, because we can never fully know it. This intangible quality pulls at our imagination and seduces us with its mystery.

Seen from the air, the dichotomy of experiencing the Lowcountry becomes apparent. With the slightest altitude one can detect the landscape beginning to unfold. It takes on a sense of balance and proportion. Rivers, islands, and marshes can be understood as interacting entities; the geography suddenly becomes manifest. On the other hand, to discern any of the elements or details is just as suddenly to abstract it again into patterns, textures, and colors which deny any scale. The Lowcountry now becomes a two-dimensional tapestry, leading us from a larger landscape to a more personal vision . . . from topography to metaphor.

Drifting in a boat down a blackwater river brings me deepest into the womb of the Lowcountry. To be pulled at random like a leaf in the current through the stillness of the swamp is to stop time while continuing to journey through space. I remain unified with the river and its gentle force, yet relationships and perspectives unfold. The river leads my senses, bathing them in a labyrinth of trees, reflections and sounds. It is the Lowcountry at its most primeval.

By comparison, the vitality of life in the Lowcountry is no more exuberant than in the water-bird nesting colonies in spring. Wading and shorebirds amass by the thousands, completely carpeting some islands. Displaced by flood tides, overheated eggs explode like firecrackers in the midday sun as the sky swirls with avian confetti. The seeming chaos, shrill cries and pungent smells make me feel inconsequential to a larger sense of purpose. Yet despite this extravaganza, this vast number of birds, it all seems so tenuous: a fragile exaggeration of life on a transitory piece of real estate.

One thing is certain: The Lowcountry cannot be taken at face value. It is changing and must evolve to tremendous pressures, both natural and human. These photographs disguise the future, for what they represent is as temporary as the next hurricane... next bulldozer... or next administration.

The Lowcountry pulls at each of us in a different manner. Lumberman, fisherman, biologist, artist, hunter, historian... whoever is connected with the land in some pursuit, loves it. Concerns may differ, even conflict, but the emotion is there. With it we listen to the land, hear its moods, and realize its natural propensities.

For the early settlers the Lowcountry was a region of irresistible beauty and boundless resources. They were driven by dreams and an aesthetic imperative. Nature, however, with its heat, storms, insects, and opaque forests quickly cut those fantasies down to size. The natural process dictated the realities of living along the coast.

Now, in a time when our culture has grown distant from the land, it requires more and more effort to relate to the earth. We risk losing our perspective. We struggle to control or suppress nature by diking, dredging, chopping, and paving. The land is the abused, but we are inevitably the victim. Whereas geography was once the shaper of history, we now reshape geography itself to suit our whims and wallets.

It is not enough to set aside Lowcountry refuges and reserves and assume they will be safe while "progress" surges at their fringes. We need to slow down and experience the Lowcountry, get closer to what is already close at hand. Most of all, we need to comprehend, without presumption, the character and spirit of the land. We need to see it humbly, for its own sake; not as a commodity, but as a community of which we are a part, as both privileged witnesses and responsible custodians.

The Lowcountry, with its inherent rhythms and subtlety, asks of us a contemplative relationship. Though it may not be a true wilderness, the Lowcountry's great virtue is that it offers a sense of wildness, and with it a chance to experience solitude, freedom, and our own individuality. This book celebrates that spirit of wildness... but it asks that in loving the Lowcountry, we not love it to death. Instead let it breathe, let it live... sustain it... and in doing so nurture our own humanness.

Thomas Blagden Jr.
Charleston, South Carolina
April, 1988

PREFACE

In the eons preceding man, the Lowcountry of South Carolina was a wildly beautiful region. Alternately covered by the sea and exposed to the sun for thousands of years at a time, the Lowcountry gives hints of her early tumultuous periods to only the most observant: fossil seashells miles inland and giant mastadon bones far out to sea indicate periods when the coastline fluctuated greatly. Today, wide white-sand beaches separate soft dunes from a dark green sea. Vast expanses of saltwater marsh lead to jungle-like barrier islands and abut inland forests that at one time blocked out the light of day.

Far inland, the mighty Appalachians rose in fury and then subsided over centuries into softer ranges. Rivers drained from these mountains through the Carolina foothills and midlands carrying sediment and depositing it on the coast, enriching the floodplains and swamps with dark soil. Everything was as nature arranged it until the coming of man.

The Indians who migrated to the Lowcountry — the Yemassee, Kiawah, Santee, Edisto, Westoes, Cherokees and others — did virtually nothing to change the environment to suit themselves, save plant small fields of maize and rig primitive fish traps. They used fire regularly to clear fields and flush game, yet little of their mark could be seen on the land. The Indians adapted to the land and lived with the flow of the seasons, taking what they needed to sustain them and no more.

Consequently, the first white men who laid eyes on the Carolinas saw a vast and beautiful wilderness full of potential for trade with England. Sailing along the coast, they beheld the endless trees and marsh. Behind the expanses of wide, waving *Spartina* marsh, golden in the fall and green in the summer, were the Southern forests. The extent of the forests was unfathomable to these men from France, Spain and England, countries long since denuded of their original forests. Each new visitor was overwhelmed at the natural abundance.

As explorers probed inland they found that the forests did not end. In their minds' eye they imagined, stretching before them, a continent with unlimited fertile land, timber, furs and precious minerals. And they were right. They had been sent across an ocean to assess the worth of this new territory and to use it. Fortified with the belief that the resources were limitless, they did not think about conservation. A few farsighted men in the mid-18th century raised the thought tentatively, but they were laughed away. Only crazy people would want to save trees and set aside sanctuaries for animals or land in the face of the extravagance and wealth of America.

Resources seemed unlimited and resources were meant to be used. European and American settlers had a country to build. They needed to clear trees for homesteads and pastures. They used the felled trees for fences, barns, wagons and tools. They burned the trees to keep warm in the unexpectedly cold Carolina winters. The giant oaks provided excellent wood for building the seaworthy sailing vessels that would carry more timber across the sea. For 300 years or so, the men and women of the Carolina Lowcountry would cut forests, clear fields, dredge swamps, dam rivers and level sand dunes until only ghostly vestiges of the original terrain could be found. It is in these remaining places, remote from the cities and usually protected by some state or federal entity, that one can feel as if time has stood still.

It wasn't until attention was drawn to the dwindling resources, starting in the last half of this century, that the collective conscience of a nation became aware that what had gone before could not continue. For the first time in the history of the United States, an attitude began developing that this land was finite and its resources should be protected and nurtured. It was almost a selfish concern, at this point, because it became clear that what is done to the land is ultimately done to ourselves. There is a saying, "Man is the only species that soils his own nest." In the Lowcountry, this consciousness took the form of protected habitats like the Santee Coastal Reserve, preserved plantations like Middleton and Magnolia, soil conservation programs, pollution control on rivers, and more.

The land itself has proved resilient. Scrappy loblolly pines tend to catch hold and grow in abandoned fields. Brambles, briars and morning glory vines can be counted on to fill ditches. Forests eventually reclaim most places, if left alone long enough. But man is doing more today than just leaving large tracts of land alone. In many instances he is caring for the land with a new tenderness and urgency. The story of the Lowcountry is the story of a land used, abused, abandoned, and now treasured. While environmental battles still go on, the region has made headway, with rivers flowing cleaner than they have in decades and much of the exploited land productive as fertile fields, forests and nature sanctuaries.

Little Pee Dee River

THE TIDAL RIVERS

Rising up from the Atlantic Ocean and stretching across to the Piedmont, the beauty of the South Carolina Lowcountry is more quiet than spectacular. It is a land of gentle contours and soft hues generously criss-crossed by rivers and streams that cascade from the North Carolina mountains and transect the state.

These rivers form the backbone and soul of the Lowcountry. To early settlers the rivers were roads. They were the major highways down which furs, timber, meat, rice, indigo and cotton were taken to markets in the port cities of Georgetown, Charleston, Beaufort and Savannah. The wealthiest planters took the choicest spots along the rivers — much like industrialists today scramble for locations near major highways and railroad routes. Waterways and harbors were the focal points of towns and eventually cities.

And so it is from the rivers that the measure of the Lowcountry should be taken. Moving slowly downriver through the Lowcountry, one can see the marks of time, the gradations of cultures that led up to today. Abandoned rice fields lie in close proximity to interstate highways, airports and malls. Wilderness areas share smog with steel mills. Plantations sit in sight of paper mills and elaborate 18th century gardens rest back-to-back with 20th century chemical plants. Nonetheless, the Lowcountry wears it well. Over the years its people have taken great pains to preserve portions of its original beauty.

Moving through the Lowcountry, its floral variety and wealth of habitats become apparent. It is a land, just like the tourism brochures boast, of magnolias and honeysuckle, whispering pines and majestic live oaks, towering cypress in black-water swamps, and rustling palmettos swaying in ocean breezes. Pine forests give way to grassy savannahs. Upland hardwoods slope to bottomland swamps. Tidal rivers open into vast salt marshes that separate the mainland from the barrier islands.

Starting at the upper part of the state, one encounters the most northerly rivers of the Lowcountry. These are the Waccamaw, Pee Dee, and Black — dark-water rivers flowing by the remains of great plantations. A short river, the Waccamaw parallels the coast briefly and then enters Winyah Bay at Georgetown. Joining it is the Black River which drains most of Sumter, Clarendon and Williamsburg counties. The two

Pee Dee rivers, the Great and the Little, form the watershed for most of Marlboro, Florence, Dillon, Marion and Horry counties. They join briefly before emptying into the Waccamaw.

Moving slowly south along the coast one encounters next the sprawling delta of the Santee River. Formed by deposits of silt, carried from the mountains, piedmont and midlands, this rich habitat stretches out leisurely between the north and south arms of the Santee. The state's largest river, the Santee forms the watershed for most of South Carolina and parts of North Carolina. In the early days of the state, it flowed freely, a great rush of mountain and piedmont water to the coast. Today, it is dammed just south of the juncture of the Congaree and Wateree to form Lake Marion. It flows much altered out of Lake Marion the remaining fifty or so miles to the coast, and enters the ocean just south of Georgetown.

The Cooper and Ashley rivers, below the Santee, are shorter coastal rivers, considered arms of the ocean. They form the watershed for most of Charleston and Berkeley counties and empty into Charleston Harbor. The peninsula between them contains the historic city of Charleston. The Cooper River has been altered, too, as part of the Santee-Cooper project, and today its flow is managed by man.

Two forks of the Edisto River drain the area between Orangeburg and Aiken, and joining together, flow through Dorchester and Colleton counties. The river divides again south of Charleston and enters the sea on either side of Edisto Island. The Ashepoo starts up around Walterboro and empties in St. Helena Sound above Hilton Head. Starting around Denmark and Barnwell, on the more westerly borders of the state, the Salkehatchie flows in the same direction, entering the Combahee which also empties into St. Helena Sound. The Coosawhatchie River empties into the larger Broad River which meets the sea in Port Royal Sound. And finally, the most southerly of the Lowcountry rivers, the Savannah divides the state from Georgia, and enters the sea about 20 miles below the city of Savannah, Georgia.

Each river is distinctive. Some follow snake-like courses with braided patterns of ox-bow lakes and islands. Some are wide and slow; others forceful and deep. Edges may have vast sweeps of floating vege-

tation, deep hardwood swamps, or rare high bluffs of oak and pine. All are tidally influenced and can feel the gentle ebb and flow of the Atlantic in their freshwater reaches, sometimes as far as thirty-five miles inland. The longer rivers that originate in the mountains have a greater surge of fresh water that keeps the salt influence of the tides at bay, closer to the mouths of the rivers. The shorter, coastal rivers feel the salt further inland.

Today, the rivers have been altered. The Savannah has been dammed three times and only her last few miles, before she enters the ocean, are free flowing. Mountain water, such as it is, is released on schedule from one massive reservoir to the next, so that the river's water quality resembles little of what it boasted in 1700. The Santee and Cooper rivers have gone through such a bizarre series of alterations by man that even today, the habitat on those rivers is continuing to change. The rivers were used as part of a WPA experiment in the 1940s to reroute water from the Santee down the Cooper. It was thought that this would increase the size and depth of the Cooper River enough to allow boat travel all the way up to Columbia. Additionally, a dam was built that provided electricity to the region.

After the completion of the Santee-Cooper lakes and dam, the great surge of fresh water from the mountains down to the mouth of the Santee was stemmed and most of it rerouted down the Cooper. The reduced flow in the Santee caused the freshwater habitat nearest the ocean to yield to saltwater habitat. Forty years later, a new problem was spotted. The South Carolina Ports Authority and U.S. Corps of Engineers decided that the increased flow down the Cooper River was causing such a buildup of silt in Charleston Harbor that shipping was being threatened. Expensive dredging could not keep up with it. A new plan was undertaken to reroute water back from the Cooper into the Santee, through a new channel. It was believed that this would reduce the amount of siltation in Charleston Harbor and solve the dredging problem. The project was completed in 1985. How the new channelization will effect siltation in Charleston Harbor is not yet known. Nor has the resultant alteration to habitat on both the Santee and Cooper Rivers been documented. There is no question, however, that both rivers will again have to adapt to new conditions.

Lowcountry rivers have been adjusting to man ever since his arrival. They have been used hard and loved well. Today there are organizations whose sole purpose is to protect South Carolina's rivers. The designation "Scenic River" is as much a term of endearment as it is a means of protection, and nowhere are the rivers more cherished than here, in the Lowcountry.

Red-tailed hawk, Savannah River

Water hyacinth and water primrose, Goose Creek, Cooper River

Santee Delta, North Santee River

Dawn on the Ashepoo River

Cattail and cordgrass, Santee River Delta

Spider-lilies, Folly Creek, Combahee River

Alligator in duckweed, Santee River

Tickseed and aster, Horseshoe Creek, Ashepoo River

Dawn on the Ashley River, Middleton Plantation

Pintail ducks, Santee River Delta impoundment, private plantation

Bald cypress and Spanish moss, Combahee River

Live oaks and resurrection fern, Dixie Plantation

UPLAND FORESTS

The pines

In the early Lowcountry forests, pine was dominant. And of the pines, the longleaf was king. Try to imagine the hundreds of thousands of acres of longleaf pine stands that greeted the early settlers as they moved inland from the coast. The aristocrat of the southern pines, the longleaf grew more than 120 feet tall and 46 or more inches in diameter. It was used for more things than any other tree in North America and vast forests fell to the ax of the lumberman. No one bothered to replant, and the fires that swept through the cutovers prevented natural reestablishment. The longleaf had other troubles. Feral hogs ranged over much of this region and destroyed millions of seedlings. Longleafs were the mainstay of the naval stores industry which used the trees for turpentine. Today the longleaf probably occupies less than a tenth of its original area. Its main stronghold is in places such as the Francis Marion National Forest where management policy is to replant longleaf after it is cut. There are also small holdings on old plantations, such as Medway in Berkeley County, where several excellent stands exist. Even those pines, however, do not equal the giants of yesterday that matured at 150 years and lived from 200 to 300 years.

The upstart who took over the longleaf's domain was the loblolly, the largest of the southern pines. Reaching heights of 170 feet with a diameter of six feet at breast height, loblollies can live for 200 years, but seldom do because of their value as timber. Loblolly grew mostly on the edges of the original southern forests; yet today it is the dominant pine one sees traveling the Lowcountry. An opportunistic stock, it thrives on sites that other species disdain, from low-lying, poorly drained soils to sterile upland fields. When agricultural fields were abandoned, for example, after the decline of cotton, the loblolly quickly reforested the fields — hence the name "old field pine." A good seeder and fast grower, loblolly can begin reproducing in 10 years, although 30 is the average. However, loblolly is the dominant pine on the Coastal Plain today mainly because of its value as pulp for use in the production of paper.

Pine forests existed, ironically, because of fire. If a pine forest is not burned periodically, the understory of hardwoods will grow up and, in a sense, take over. This is known in the scientific community as "natural succession." In this process, the pines grow first and fastest in the open fields. As they get taller, an understory develops of both pine and hardwoods, such as oak and hickory trees. The pines are poor competitors and, as the trees grow, the pine seedlings die due to lack of sunlight in the shaded forest. The hardwood seedlings fare better because their broad leaves can absorb the sun they need. The original pine stands mature, as do the cohabiting hardwoods, and they will exist side by side for decades if not disturbed. Eventually the pines will die and leave the longer-lived hardwoods in what is called a climax forest. That is how the forest will stand until either fire comes to destroy the hardwoods, or man cuts down the trees. If, on the other hand, periodic fires kill off the hardwood understory, the mature pines can withstand the brief flames, and continue to grow. Today, man still uses fire in a controlled fashion to maintain the abundance of pine found in the Lowcountry.

Fire preserved the "pine" character of the Lowcountry woodlands, yet fire also decimated the forests. The early settlers believed that "firings" would flush game or kill the ever-present mosquitos and chiggers in the summertime. Very often, efforts at controlled burns got out of hand. Vast forests became infernos; homes, fields and livestock were destroyed. Millions of board feet of the great southern forests were lost over the decades to fire.

The first extensive commercial use of the Lowcountry's pines came in the early 1700s. Around this time men began to use the longleaf pines of the Carolina Lowcountry for turpentine and pine tar. Turpentine is found in the resin canals of the inner bark and sapwood of various coniferous trees. It produces spirits of turpentine, an essential oil, and resin when it is distilled. The oil was necessary to the paint and varnish industry, and the resin was used in the manufacture of soap, varnish and paint. Pine tar is the crude liquid that drips from the wood during slow combustion. Pitch is the product obtained when tar is boiled or burned. Pitch was used chiefly for caulking wooden sailing vessels and tar was used to coat the rigging of the ships.

Pine trees were cut and burned slowly in great earthern pits, called tar kilns, to extract the tar. Turpentining, on the other hand, was done on live trees. It was hard on the forest: hacking and bleeding trees, wounding but not quite killing them. Trees were bled continuously for several years — up to ten — as long as they continued to produce turpentine. The naval stores industry tapered off with the advent of metal hulled ships and steam and diesel power; turpentining continues only on a limited basis today.

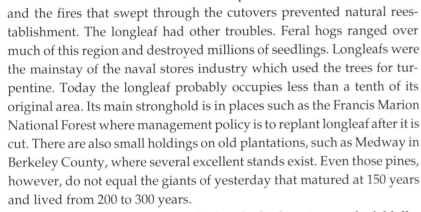

By the 1800s, southern forests were seeing an unprecedented amount of activity. They were cleared for homesteads and eventually cities, for farming, and especially for rice and cotton planting. Land speculators from outside the region picked up these lands for a fraction of their prewar value, taking advantage of destitute southerners, broken by the war, and plantation owners whose crops were no longer lucrative. Lumbermen, especially, rushed to cut virgin tracts of timber and to snatch up fields that had grown over in pine. Other outsiders recognized the old plantation sites as valuable hunting reserves.

Around 1908 a development in the pulp industry led to a new wave of timbering. Prior to this time, pines could not be used for pulp because of the resin in the wood. The new sulfate process removed resin, allowing pines to be used in the paper industry. Fast-growing loblolly became the tree of choice to replant. Pines were felled from the barrier islands to the mountains. World War I fostered another assault when mills were pressured to step up production for wartime needs such as wooden cargo ships, training camps and warehouses. By 1925 the once great southern pine forests had been laid waste.

Today, new forests have risen from the stumps and the ashes. Timber companies revised forestry practices and have planted millions of trees. Farmers began practicing soil conservation techniques. Farsighted men and women began placing large tracts of land in reserves and sanctuaries. The great plantations bought up for timber and hunting became wildlife refuges and provide timber resources on a continual basis.

Yet the pine forests of the Lowcountry, especially where they are cultivated on timber company land and in the National Forests, have a sameness born of efficiency. Understories, burned repeatedly to keep out competing hardwoods, are covered with soft brown pine needles or sometimes lime-green ferns. They are beautiful in their own way, with the warm smell of pine straw and the quiet buzzing of pine warblers in the tree tops. And yet they are bland. Fortunately, there are habitats within these pine forest which lend excitement and drama to the plainness of the pine monocultures.

Pitcher-plant bogs, evergreen-shrub bogs and pond-cypress ponds

Pitcher-plant bogs are some of the most unusual habitat you will find as you move inland from the rivers. Found within the pine forest, several good examples are in the Francis Marion National Forest, the Santee Coastal Reserve and the Webb Wildlife Center in Hampton County. No other Lowcountry habitat has such an exciting array of plant life as the pitcher-plant bog. Here one finds the true exotics of the region — carnivorous plants, adapted over centuries to capture and digest their unwitting insect meals. And here, too, are the reigning beauties of the flower kingdom, Lowcountry orchids, as beautiful as their tropical brethren.

Bogs have no drainage, or if they do, it is a slow seepage into the ground, usually stopped by a hardpan underneath. Bogs have an acid soil and a low level of nutrients in the muddy waters. In this environment plants have had to adapt to water-logged soils with a low oxygen content. Thus they have narrow leaves and thick cuticles to reduce the rate of water loss from leaves into the atmosphere.

The carnivores, found almost exclusively in bogs, are complex and beautiful plants that have developed an ingenious system of capturing nutrients and minerals lacking in the bog. The common carnivorous plants found in Lowcountry bogs include pitcher plants — tall and slender pitcher-shaped flora that lure insects to the mouth of the "pitcher" where they slip down and cannot climb out. Innocent-looking bladderworts and butterworts also snare insects, as do tiny sun dews and endangered Venus flytraps. These plants are complete, miniature systems that have survived over the ages, seemingly by their wits. Starting in the spring, a showy procession of wildflowers brightens the bogs with sun bonnets and orchids such as grass pink, spreading pogonia, yellow-fringed orchid and ladies' tresses.

Like the pine forest, pitcher-plant bogs require periodic fire to maintain themselves. Fire destroys competing vegetation, but leaves underground rhizomes and rootstalks unharmed, allowing bog plants to regenerate robustly in the spring. If competing vegetation is not removed, either by fire or cutting, shrubs such as the wax myrtle and sweet pepperbush invade the bog community. As these "woody" shrubs take root, they contribute, through their decay, to the soil layer and slowly decrease the wet nature of the bog through transpiration. Eventually, new and different species take root in the dryer soil, with the bog being replaced by a woody shrub community, and ultimately, a forest.

Another type of bog, the evergreen-shrub bog, is often referred to as a pocosin, an Indian word meaning "swamp on a hill." And that is an apt description of this habitat, home to the few remaining black bears in the coastal region. These evergreen-shrub bogs are dense thickets dominated by shrubs such as sweetbay, red bay, loblolly bay, fetterbush, pepperbush, gallberry and leatherleaf. Evergreen-shrub bogs also depend on periodic fires to maintain themselves.

Yet another habitat of the pine forest is the pond-cypress pond, found in depressions where water sits throughout the year. The dominant tree in this community is the pond cypress, a much smaller tree than its close relative, the bald cypress. Swamp gum can codominate with this tree or be completely absent. Dahoon holly, buttonbush and titi shrubs form a subcanopy. Wading birds find this environment excellent for nesting. Herons, ibis and egrets build noisy rookeries here and migrating waterfowl depend on these ponds as important stopovers.

A system of mysterious depressions, called Carolina Bays, is found with regularity in the pine forests. These depressions, where many of the evergreen-shrub bogs can be found, have left scientists wondering about their origin. Naturalists were aware of the existence of Carolina Bays as early as 1700, but no one realized their extent until an aerial photograph in 1930 revealed that there were half a million of these depressions scattered along the east coast from Maryland to Georgia. One theory attributes these intriguing land formations to a meteor shower. Henry Savage, author of *The Mysterious Carolina Bays*, was not guilty of hyperbole in describing them. They are staggering to contemplate: half a million elliptical depressions deep in the earth — one four miles long, others a hundred yards across — spread across the Atlantic Coastal Plain from Maryland to Georgia. If indeed the Carolina Bays resulted from a meteor shower, it would have rocked the eastern seaboard in a convulsion of fire and brimstone. However, little scientific evidence exists to support this theory.

The hardwoods

On either side of the river, one will see interspersed between the pine forests, the hardwood, or deciduous forests. While all trees shed their leaves, deciduous trees shed them all in the fall. Hardwood forests make

up possibly 15 to 20 percent of the forested acreage of the Lowcountry, a land dominated by pine. Yet they are home to the greatest wealth and diversity of trees and provide critical habitat for deer, turkeys, bobcats, foxes, squirrels, rabbits, quail and other Lowcountry inhabitants.

Generally called upland hardwood forests, these habitats fall into three "phases," mostly differentiated by soil moisture. "Dry" forests are made up of oaks: turkey oak, bluejack oak, blackjack oak and post oak. "Intermediate" phase forests have sweetgum, white oak, willow oak, laural oak, shagbark hickory, persimmon, blackgum and some loblolly.

The most varied of the three forest types, the southern mixed hardwood forest, is often referred to as the "rich" phase. It boasts beech, southern magnolia, holly, flowering dogwood, sparkleberry, spruce pine, tulip tree, swamp chestnut oak, silverbell and a host of others. Here the wildflowers are most abundant with trillium, white bloodroot, broadleaved mayapple, cranefly orchid, wild geraniums, wood sorrel, wild ginger, and the beautiful wild azalea.

Hardwood forests have been reduced in size over the centuries because of their economic value. White oak was suited for making barrels and live oak for building ships; dogwood for looms; black cherry and black walnut were superb for furniture and cabinets. And, the hardwood forests have been reduced in size because their habitats have been replanted in pine. Today, despite intensive development on the coast, there are efforts toward protecting this once bountiful Lowcountry legacy. Forty percent of South Carolina's coastal acreage is in one type of protected status or another. Much of the coast is preserved in such tracts as the Yawkey Wildlife Reserve, the Belle Baruch Institute, the Santee Coastal Reserve, Cape Romain, Capers Island, Magnolia, Middleton and Cypress gardens, Bear Island Refuge, Edisto State Park, Hunting Island, St. Phillips Island and the Savannah Wildlife Refuge. The refuge parks of the Lowcountry are islands in a sea of development.

Red maple near Green Pond

Lichen and resurrection fern on live oak bark, St. Phillips Island

Overleaf: Pond cypress, Francis Marion National Forest

Longleaf pine forest with bracken fern, Rochelle Plantation

Bobcat running, Poco Sabo Plantation

Pines and dogwood, Brookgreen Gardens

Venus flytrap, Cartwheel Bay

Pine forest at sunset, Francis Marion National Forest

White-tail deer and pine forest, Georgetown County

Forest floor in autumn, Dixie Plantation

Sweet pitcher plants and ferns, Santee Coastal Reserve

Meadow beauties, Francis Marion National Forest

Live oaks and dogwood blossoms, near the Wando River

Bald cypress in dawn mist, Page's Millpond, Lake View

SWAMP FORESTS AND FRESHWATER WETLANDS

Swamp forests occur on the flood plains of the Lowcountry's slow-moving rivers. Stretching out on either side of the river, sometimes for a mile or more, these flood plains hold the overflow when spring rains and mountain snow melts cause rivers to rise. Flooding lasts for a couple days, and subsides, but the forest floor holds the water for months at a time.

The true swamp forest or bald cypress-tupelo gum forest, and its neighbor, the bottomland hardwood forest, constitute the Lowcountry's lowland hardwood forests.

While the bottomland hardwood forest is not a swamp, it sits in and around swamp forests on slightly higher elevations. It too, is periodically flooded, though not as long as the swamp forest. The little bit of difference in elevation causes a marked change in which trees grow in each habitat. The bottomland hardwood forest is an incredibly rich habitat because alluvial soil, washed down from the mountains and piedmont, settles out as the waters hit the flood plain. More than 30 different species of tree can be found in the bottomland hardwood forest including cottonwood, water hickory, pumpkin ash, overcup oak, winged elm, black willow, and sugarberry.

But it is the swamp forests of the Carolina Lowcountry that capture the imagination and give a sense of wilderness in a trampled land. Indeed, the remaining ones are true examples of how portions of this land looked at one time. In the areas of deepest flooding, the swamp forest is most beautiful. Towering bald cypress, draped in Spanish moss; tupelo gums and swamp gums are reflected in the black water. Each has adapted to the saturated environment by developing swollen bases, called buttresses, that give the trees steady footing in the wet soil. Cypress trees are surrounded by knobby protrusions called "knees" whose function was once believed to aid in gaseous exchange. Scientists no longer believe this is the case, but are unsure what purpose the knees serve.

On the slightly elevated sites are understories of smaller trees, their delicate branches forming a green, lace-like network. Ash, red maple, American elm and water elm can be found here, with laurel oak, sweet gum and water locust. Rooted on the hammocks and cypress knees are shrubs such as wax myrtle, fetterbush, buttonbush, swamp dogwood, Virginia willow and storax. Resurrection ferns decorate trunks and branches while poison ivy and smilax vines form thickets on rotted logs. In this dark, cool environment can be found brilliant flashes of Cardinal flower and other wildflowers like arrow arrum, golden club, milkweed and obedient plant.

The swamps were at first inhospitable to development and agriculture because they stayed flooded for long periods of time. Profitable timbering was out of the question because there was no cost-effective way to log timber in the soggy location. Originally, the only cutting done was of select trees in the swamps, mostly bald cypress, with giant stumps left to testify to their size. Later, the swamp forests were extensively cut to make room for rice planting, and then again as forestry equipment improved.

Remnants of original-growth swamp forest can still be found in the Lowcountry. The very best example is in Beidler Forest/Four Holes Swamp Sanctuary near Harleyville, South Carolina, some forty-five miles northwest of Charleston. Four-Holes Swamp was bought by northern timber barons and escaped even the selective cutting done in most swamps. It has the world's largest remaining tract of original growth-bald cypress and tupelo gum — some 1,700 acres — with trees thought to be as old as 600 years. An outstanding example of what this country looked like before man altered it, this river swamp is part of a 5,464-acre river forest protected as part of National Audubon's Wildlife Sanctuary system and co-owned with the Nature Conservancy. The tract sits within a 60-mile-long, mile-and-a-half wide swamp system. One can take night walks in spring down the boardwalk, and listen to barred owls and night herons raise their eerie voices in the dark. In the day, jewel-like prothonotary warblers flash through the cypress knees, and in the dark pools alligators rise silently to the surface.

So long believed ugly and fearsome, the swamp forest is now loved for its beauty, rarity, and for its function as valuable habitat for wild turkeys, bobcats, deer, owls and ducks. Almost all the wading birds build their rookeries in or near the swamp. The swamp is also recognized today for how it interacts with the rest of the environment. A swamp provides food for animals that inhabit the surrounding uplands. Detritus, a composition of decayed plants, forms in the swamp and is an important base for the food chain when it is eventually washed into coastal estuaries. The swamp acts as a storage system, slowly releasing water in time of drought into rivers and estuaries. It modifies temperatures and the moisture content of the lower atmosphere, buffering freezing conditions and providing a refuge for animals that might not survive the winter.

In the 18th century, the tidal freshwater swamp forests were cut the length and breadth of Lowcountry rivers to plant rice, a crop that would contribute substantially toward the economy and culture of the Lowcountry. If any one image has come to be associated with the Lowcountry, it would be the plantation. Over the decades, novels and movies such as *Gone With The Wind* have held up an impossibly beautiful image of the prewar South, of eternally feminine and beguiling women, gallant and dashing men, expansive fields, flush with the snowy caps of the cotton plant or golden and waving with the ripening rice.

Medway, Hampton, Hobcaw Barony, Drayton Hall, Middleton, Fairfield, The Wedge, Harrietta, Prospect Hill, Hopseewee Plantation and a hundred others exist today, though they are only a fraction of the number that lined the banks of the rivers and filled the Carolina backwoods. Not one is operating as a rice or cotton plantation today. Instead, owners maintain them as private residences, manage them as hunting preserves, timberlands or farm them through aquaculture. Only one Lowcountry owner is known to plant rice, just enough to get a taste of the one-time world-famous Carolina Gold Rice. Where the old rice dikes broke and natural succession followed, many of the rice fields have returned to swamp forests. A fortunate few historic homes have been preserved as beautifully cultivated gardens, open to visitors to contemplate what it must have been like.

The rivers were the single most important factor in growing rice, which requires fresh water, and must be flooded and drained at critical periods during its growth. They provided the fresh water and, being close to the Atlantic Ocean, they also provided tidal surges — some as far as thirty-five miles inland. Through a series of ingenious dikes, wooden gates, trunks and reservoirs, the planters used these tidal fluctuations to provide flooding and draining that helped rice grow so successfully here.

Historians divide the rice era into two distinct periods. Beginning just before the 1700s and lasting up to the end of the American Revolution, plantations were established on the inland swamps. Here they grew Carolina Gold Rice from a seed brought in from Madagascar around 1685. The rice got its name from the color of the outer hull and it was renowned world-wide because of its excellent quality. By 1700, more rice was being produced in the Carolinas than there were ships to transport it. But the inland planters had problems with their system of growing rice. The reservoirs were a source of uncertainty and consternation. They were subject to droughts and freshets. Planters began to see that they could get the same flooding and draining effects with a dependable regularity on the freshwater ends of the tidal rivers. Starting roughly around 1740, the planters began to abandon the cleared inland swamps for the tidal rivers, initiating the second and greater period of the rice plantations. For the next century the swamp forests were leveled and rice was grown along tidal rivers as far north as the Cape Fear River in North Carolina and as far south as northern Florida.

Three major factors contributed to the decline of rice in the Lowcountry. After the Civil War, while many freed slaves stayed on the plantations and continued to cultivate rice, many others did not, choosing to work for themselves or to hire out their labor for less onerous jobs. The skilled workers necessary to grow rice were being lost by the planters. Around 1880 and later, rice was being grown more economically in the West. Finally, in 1910 and 1911, two massive hurricanes swept through the Lowcountry, destroying crops and breaking dikes. They were the final blow to the great era of rice planting in the Lowcountry.

Today, the former rice fields have taken on a new importance, and have become the focus of heated debate. When dikes fell into disrepair, water rushed in, and in many cases, the fields followed natural succession and returned to river swamps. Where dikes were maintained, however, the impounded fresh waters became feeding grounds for ducks from the Northeast, migrating along the Atlantic flyway. This made for great hunting in the fall and winter. Impounded wetlands today are some of the most beautiful freshwater marshes in the Lowcountry, providing a choice habitat for shorebirds, herons, egrets, woodstorks, alligators, otters, ospreys, ducks and many other species of wildlife.

Environmentalists, state agencies, wildlife officials and private land owners are at odds over how these former rice fields should be managed.

Some owners want to rebuild the dikes, install flood gates, and manage the fields for waterfowl. Others want to try their hand at aquaculture, using the impoundments to grow shrimp and blue crabs. Some environmentalists want the lands strictly left alone to perform the natural functions they have been serving for the past 75 years. Owners who want to reimpound their lands counter that many diverse species of wildlife will benefit and that impoundments, while good for waterfowl, are good for the environment as a whole. Scientists cannot agree, and politics has become no small part of the battle, as the question of private property rights clashes with state claims over ownership of the wetlands. The debate rages in and out of court — leave the lands to reach their normal ecological climax or manage them toward other ends?

"After the Civil War, the South was broke," says Jack Leland, descendent of a plantation owner and a retired newspaper columnist from Charleston. "The Northerners flooded in here to buy up the acreage of destitute plantation owners. It was the end of an era. Many called it the second Yankee invasion. But in a way, it was a great blessing. The men in the 1880s and '90s bought up the great tracts of land and restored many of the old houses and preserved, intact, land that otherwise would certainly have been lost."

Leland cites the Santee Coastal Reserve, 23,000 acres of protected marsh and woods that at one time was contained in several different plantations. In protected status since it was given to the Nature Conservancy and the South Carolina Heritage Trust Program in 1974, the Santee Coastal Reserve is perhaps the best single example of how some Lowcountry land made the transition from wilderness, to plantation, to wilderness again. Situated on the South Santee River, the land was acquired by Joseph Blake who worked some 900 slaves on several thousand acres. This tract later felt the blows of the Civil War and the loss of slaves. The plantation house was finally detroyed by federal gun boats from the river and eventually northerners bought it as a hunting reserve and made it into the Santee Gun Club in 1898. President Grover Cleveland was one of the early members. Over the years the members expanded the Gun Club's holdings to the present 23,000 acres.

The Santee-Cooper project and the damming of the Santee River in the 1940s caused the great marshes at the mouth of the Santee to lose the freshwater so critical to the production of waterfowl food, and conse-

quently, to waterfowl hunting. Club members handled the crisis by reverting to the methods of the early rice planters — they built more dikes and strengthened the old ones. When the land was deeded to the Nature Conservancy, 100 miles of dikes were standing strong, maintaining the freshwater impoundments.

Freshwater marshes hold a diversity of plant life, and are a wildflower paradise from early spring through summer. Cordgrass, southern wild rice, cattail, saw grass and beard grass highlight the vegetation. In shallow spots, ferns and orchids such as fragrant ladies' tresses grow. Vines are prevalent and blue iris and rose mallow grow in abundance.

The Santee Coastal Reserve embodies, in one place, all the natural diversity and cultural remnants that make up the Lowcountry. Its habitats include Carolina bays, marshes, pines, hardwoods, and barrier islands, a cypress swamp, bogs and old rice fields. Its history is typical of the tidewater life: first the natural state, then rice planting, wealth, destitution, purchase by Northerners and reacquisition by conservation-minded natives. It holds a diversity of wildlife, some of it endangered and found only in such protected places. On the reserve one can see deer, feral hogs, raccoons, bobcats, foxes, otters and alligators. Thousands of ducks visit each year, and there are nesting colonies of endangered red-cockaded woodpeckers. In the cypress swamps of the old reserve there are rookeries of ibis, heron, egret and anhingas, species of birds that are fast losing places to call home. The fish hawk, or osprey, reigns king of the preserve, with massive nests atop the tall cypress trees. The endangered American bald eagle can·be found here, coming back strong along the South Carolina coast because of these protected habitats and intensive management practices. Likewise, loggerhead turtles nest safely on the beaches of Murphy and Cedar islands, the two protected barrier islands on the reserve.

The legacy of the plantation system is a strange one indeed. The myopic devotion to the monocultures of rice and cotton led to the downfall of the South in the Civil War. With all money, labor and energy going into these crops, the region failed to develop industry and to incorporate divergent cultures as the North was doing. Both rice and cotton plantations eventually crumbled for a variety of reasons. Yet some of these same tracts of land, held intact and preserved, are the Lowcountry's remaining "wilderness."

Water-lily pads, private plantation, Santee River Delta

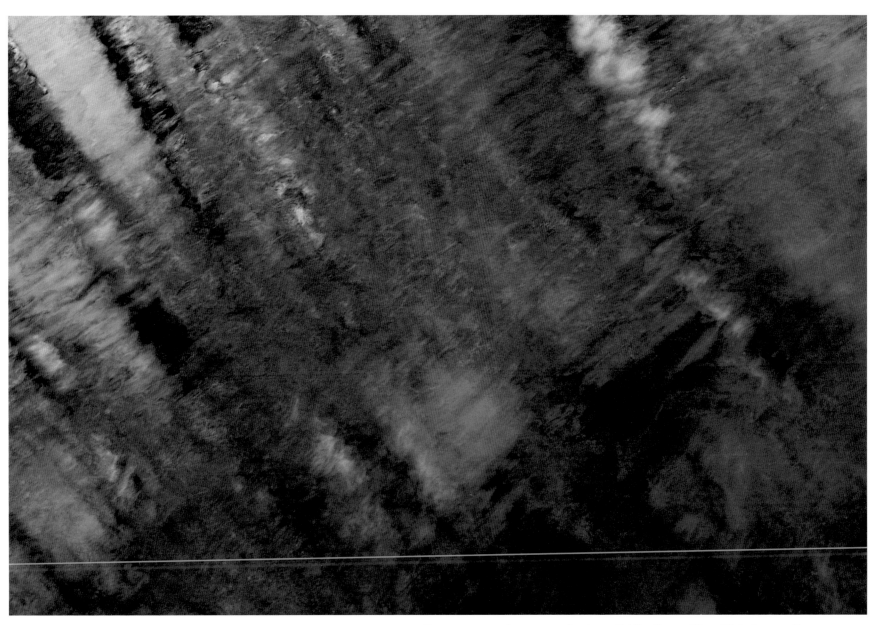

Swamp gum and cypress reflections, Beidler Forest / Four Hole Swamp Sanctuary

Floating bladderwort and bald cypress, Cypress Gardens

Impoundment, South Island, Yawkey Wildlife Center

Cypress needles and reflections, Fairlawn Plantation

Wood stork, Santee Coastal Reserve

Blue iris, Santee Coastal Reserve

Bald cypress swamp with Spanish moss in autumn, private plantation, Horry County

Blue-wing teal and pintail, Bear Island Wildlife Management Area

Atamasco-lilies, Francis Marion National Forest

From upper left: great horned owl, Carolina parakeet (extinct), Carolina parakeet (extinct), blue-winged teal, red-winged blackbird, purple gallinule, and glossy ibis

Cattails and water-lily, Savannah National Wildlife Refuge

Botany Island, tidal creeks and spartina marsh, North Edisto River

THE SALT MARSH

Before one reaches the sea, one enters the vast expanse of the salt marshes. On the South Carolina coast, more than 500,000 acres of estuaries and marshland separate the mainland from barrier islands. The Charleston Harbor estuary, including the Ashley, Cooper and Wando rivers contains about 10 percent of the state's coastal marsh. No other habitat on earth, except perhaps that of the tropical rainforests, is as prolific as marsh. Mud flats and tidal creeks, alternately flooded and drained, act as nurseries for two-thirds of the world's marine fisheries, and three-quarters of the Atlantic coast's fish, shellfish and crustaceans. Shrimp, clam, crab and other fisheries account for a 12 million dollar industry dependent on South Carolina's estuaries, which include Winyah Bay, St. Helena and Port Royal sounds, in addition to Charleston Harbor.

Someone new to the area might think a marsh at low tide is repugnant, but it is valued for its aesthetics. Open, waving spaces of marsh grass, golden in the fall and green in the summer, bleed off into the brilliant blues of tidal creeks. The trill of the tiny long-billed marsh wren mingles with the cackle of the clapper rail. Even the odd, rank smell of pluff mud at low tide — hydrogen sulfide gas released from decaying matter — is cherished by people who have grown up with it and have a proprietary feeling about it. Lots with even a view of the marsh command high prices in today's real estate market.

The marshes are most valuable for the critical habitat they provide — not just for commercial fishing species — but for all the creatures of land and sea that need this environment to survive. They are a foundation for marine life and a host of other species that live in and around the estuary. Every six hours, give or take a few minutes, the tide floods, covering marsh grass and mud flats, flushing the marsh with nutrients and allowing shellfish to feed; carrying in fish and other sea creatures who feed and mate. When the tide recedes, shorebirds, raccoons and others come to forage on the mud flats.

Beneath the surface waters of the estuaries exists an incalculable variety of life. Detritus forms the bottom of a food chain culminating with man. In between are worms, shrimp, oysters, clams, crabs, mussels, menhaden, bass, flounder, gulls, terns, ibis, egrets, porpoises, seaturtles and sharks.

Mud flats, exposed at low tide, are as deceptive as the flat surface of the estuary. Millions of life-and-death battles go on in the tidal flats at each low tide; the exchanges of energy are endless. Biologists estimate some one million fiddler crabs may live on an acre of mudflat, burrowing in to escape wading birds and mammals. It is quite a sight to see a mud bank with thousands of fiddler claws moving up and down in synchronization; the males waving their elongated claws to catch the attention of females during mating season. They mate and lay eggs, fight and die, consume and are consumed by higher lifeforms. In doing so, they exemplify a cycle that never stops in the marsh.

Some plants have adapted to this constant flooding and draining of salt water. Two types of marsh grass, *Spartina alterniflora* and *Spartina patens*, sea aster, black needle rush and glasswort thrive in this environment. They undulate in the sea winds, dying, decaying and beginning the process that will feed life forms such as crustaceans and invertebrates. These, in turn, are food for the birds: the plovers, willets, sandpipers, terns and gulls that probe for them with their long bills. Noisy black and white oystercatchers are abundant on the mud flats, using their outrageously orange bills to sever the muscles of the oyster and get inside the shell. In fall and winter, one can spot the ducks: hooded mergansers and buffleheads, pintails and greenwinged teals, tiny grebes and common moorhens. Warblers, sparrows, wrens, buntings and swallows comb the marshes for insects and seeds.

Wading birds especially, whose rookeries have been declining on the east coast for years, need estuaries as feeding grounds. Drum Island in Charleston Harbor and Pumpkinseed Island in Winyah Bay have been recorded as hosting 30,000 or more pairs of nesting ibis, egrets and herons.

The marshes shelter the coast from harsh storms that blow from the sea. The vast flushing action of the tides in the marshes filters and assimilates wastes. Unfortunately, the natural cleansing action of estuaries has been abused and many have begun to feel the stresses of unacceptable levels of pollution. Through waste management plans, authorities are trying to protect and preserve these critical habitats. Once considered an unattractive wasteland, the marshes and estuaries are now protected everywhere by federal and state legislation.

Great egrets, Pumpkinseed Island, Winyah Bay

Sunrise over Folly Island

Marbled godwits, oystercatchers, turnstones, knots, and dowitchers, Cape Romain National Wildlife Refuge

Tidal mud banks and oyster beds, Port Royal Sound (aerial)

Huspah Creek off Whale Branch and the Coosaw River

Spartina marsh near St. Phillips Island (aerial)

Overleaf: White ibis,
Pumpkinseed Island,
Winyah Bay

65

Glasswort, spartina, and black needle rush, South Island, Yawkey Wildlife Center

Marsh islands, St. Helena Sound

Mud flats at low tide, sunrise, Edisto Island

American oystercatchers on oyster shell bank, Cape Romain National Wildlife Refuge

Pelicans over the front beach, Capers Island Preserve

THE BARRIER ISLANDS

Perhaps as a nation we are too traditionally optimistic, confident of avoiding or conquering all disasters.
We choose to stand, express ourselves freely in our development and fight the natural forces with our engineering genius. The barrier islands, as their name implies, have barred the sea from the mainland.
We have become so confident in our technology that engineers now propose their own barriers to bar the ocean from the islands.

"The Beaches are Moving,"
by Wallace Kaufman and Orrin Pilkey, 1979

The salt marshes reach outward for the sea. But there is one obstacle between them and the sea — the long, low stretches of land just off the coast, known as barrier islands. Building over eons, the barriers stand watch over the mainland. Here the wind and waves meet the first line of defense — hence the name barriers. White sand dunes and scrubby forests take the first assaults of wind and waves, and their peculiar toughness is an adaptation to this environment.

Barrier islands, perhaps more than any other habitat in the Lowcountry, are dynamic landforms constantly in a state of flux. Government and private individuals have spent millions of dollars in attempts to get barriers to stand still, and their efforts would be amusing if it were not that so much tax money has been spent in folly. Barrier islands are forever changing, while remaining, more or less, the same size in roughly the same place. In the ceaseless movement of wind, waves and sand, there is an extravagant exchange of energy, and it changes the shape and face of the island. "The whole island, from sound to ocean, moves with the beach, changing shape and position," write Kaufman and Pilkey. "Not only do all parts of the island move, but these smaller motions are part of a much larger one — the island rolling backward over itself, retreating in the face of rising sea level." Geologists suspected this giant rolling motion for years, but it was only proven in the late 1960s.

What the islands cannot defend against is man determined to subdue them. The single greatest threat to barrier islands and beaches today is man's drive to put up houses as close to the beach as possible, and then to stop the beach from moving. But the ocean will make the final determination.

There was a time when some of the barrier islands, and the sea islands directly behind, were cut over for crops — at first for indigo, and later for the tremendously lucrative sea island cotton. Cotton had been growing in the South as long as there had been settlers, but was not grown on a commercial scale until the vexing problem of separating seeds from the fiber was solved. It was particularly difficult to remove the seeds from greenseed cotton, grown primarily inland. It was easier to remove the seeds from sea island cotton, called blackseed cotton, which was a much silkier, finer type of fiber, in greater demand and bringing a higher price.

After the invention of the gin, however, greenseed, or short staple cotton became the basis of the Southern economy. But there would be a price to pay for such easy fortunes. Planters depleted their soils of minerals and nutrients and did nothing to restore them. The boll weevil hit with a vengeance and there was no protecting against nor recovering from it.

Where barrier islands have reverted to their natural state man can still enjoy almost primeval conditions. North, South and Cat islands on the Yawkey Preserve, Murphy's Island on the Santee Coastal Reserve, Bull's Island on Cape Romain, Capers Island, St. Phillips — all are barrier islands that stand much as they did 300 years ago.

Here it takes a special type of tree and plant to withstand the harsh combination of moving sand, salt water and pounding winds. Red bay, southern red cedar, yaupon, loblolly pine and wild olive have established themselves in between the dominant live oaks. Sable or cabbage palmetto, the state tree, is the first indicator of the Lowcountry's subtropical southern climate and adds an air of almost jungle-like quality to the maritime forest. One introduced tree, the Chinese tallow or "popcorn" tree, has taken root on the barriers in the understories, adding vibrant red and yellow colors in the fall. In the winter, their seeds resemble popcorn, hence the common name. Wildflowers flourish in the open fields in the springtime. Yellow coreopsis, a daisy-like flower, mixes with bursts of purple phlox and white-topped sedge, creating waving fields of color.

Live oak is dominant here, standing alone in its majesty and quiet beauty. Near the ocean it is twisted and gnarled. Slightly inland it grows to magnificent size, stretching its heavy limbs so far that from their very weight, they touch down, ground themselves, and bound back up again.

Live oak symbolizes the Old South and the Lowcountry. One can see it on the fashionable logos of land developments and on classy bank brochures. *Quercus virginiana*, a member of the beech family, is found from tidewater Virginia southward to North Carolina, South Carolina, Georgia, Florida, and into the Gulf states as far as Texas. Growing 40 to 50 feet tall, it has a squat trunk and a wide-spreading crown of almost oriental appearance. Giants of the species grow as tall as 70 feet with trunks 20 feet in circumference and crowns that throw a shadow out 150 feet.

In the 17th and 18th centuries, however, live oaks were appreciated mainly for their unique properties in respect to sailing ships. In *Live Oaking: Southern Timber for Tall Ships*, Virginia Steele Wood recorded the history of how these trees opened the commercial timber industry to the Lowcountry. While the gnarled look of the tree is beautiful, it rendered it practically useless for most woodworking because of its extreme toughness and durability. But it was these same traits that were useful to shipwrights, who needed a durable wood, resistant to rot, with a variety of curves and shapes to fit a ship. These natural curves allowed shipwrights to build strong ships without having to use weaker crossgrain cuts.

Live oak was the timber of choice in the construction of British ships which carried goods to and from the colonies. Later, it was used to build American ships that defeated the British ships, and then, finally, to build ships that accommodated the burgeoning commerce between the new nation, England and the rest of the world. Before 1700, and for more than a hundred years, craftsmen were brought from the Northeast to live on barriers and inland forests and cut the oaks on Bull's Island and Hilton Head, Daufauskie and Hunting islands — all the great barriers. They built naval vessels, whaleships, packets and clipper ships which sailed all over the world. These "live oakers" did a remarkable job of depleting the Lowcountry of her live oak forests.

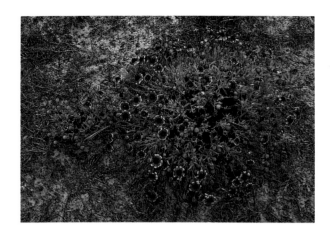

Yet it was live oaking that spawned one of the first American attempts at conservation. Agents of the United States Navy, on a fact-finding mission to evaluate the remaining timber suitable for Naval vessels in the early 1800s, came back with an alarming report — more than half of the accessible timber along the coast had disappeared. Live oak was stripped sometimes as far as fifteen miles up rivers.

From this situation two concepts emerged: establishing reserves for live oaks or developing live oak nurseries. The nurseries were actually established and hundreds of thousands of live oaks were planted. But the projects were lost in the political shuffle, received no funding, and were eventually abandoned, thus killing the first major attempt in America to preserve a depleted resource.

With the advent of steel ships the demand for live oaks decreased and for a period they were not rigorously harvested. Today, there is no commercial market for the Lowcountry's live oaks, except for the lucky developer who finds them in a parcel and incorporates them into his development. The grandest live oaks still stand today on many of the old plantations and they have come back in full force on the barriers, especially those that are in protected status.

Protected barriers will remain in their natural state and be available for those who wish to know what this habitat looked like before man altered it. "Barrier islands and barrier spits, with water behind and before, could not exist without the beach," write Kaufman and Pilkey. "Marshes, giant dunes, forests — they are made and constantly remade out of the beach sand. The well-being of the beach is the very existence of the island. The islands have existed for fifteen thousand years, but not in the same place or of the same substance. We occupy the barrier islands like people who have built cities on the backs of giant sea turtles. Like all reptiles, turtles must breathe, but we so enjoy our perch we will not tolerate the beast moving even to keep a footing in water shallow enough for it to raise its head."

Plume grass and palmetto, Hunting Island State Park

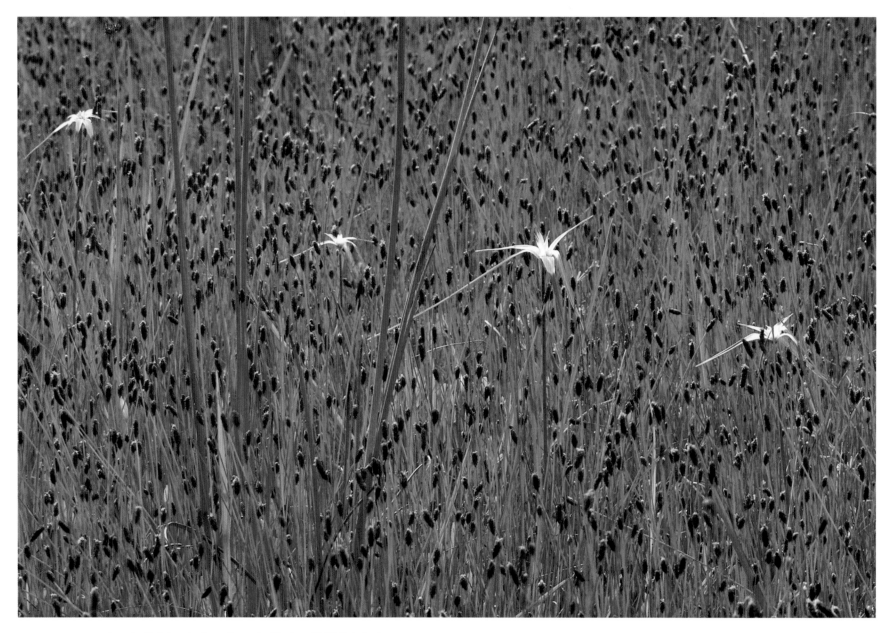

White-top sedge, Bulls Island, Cape Romain National Wildlife Refuge

Chinese tallow, Bulls Island, Cape Romain National Wildlife Refuge

Decaying myrtle, Capers Island Preserve

Oaks in surf at dawn, Capers Island Preserve

Tallow leaves and reflections, Bulls Island, Cape Romain National Wildlife Refuge

Palm trunk with windblown coreopsis and phlox, Sullivans Island

Coreopsis and phlox, Hilton Head Island

Osprey and nest, Capers Island Preserve

Chinese tallow and palm forest, Bulls Island, Cape Romain National Wildlife Refuge

Black gum leaves and palm tree, Palmetto Islands County Park

Cabbage palms with burned trunks, Hunting Island State Park

Sea oats, dunes and storm clouds, Folly Beach

Moonrise, Hunting Island State Park

THE COASTAL EDGE

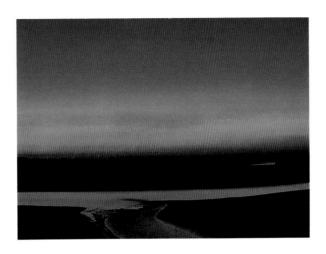

Ultimately, the Lowcountry is a child of the sea. Its mystique and ineffable beauty is seen and sensed down the rivers and across the fields and forested lands leading up to the sea. But they are largely indicators of what is to come, for the full force of the Lowcountry's beauty is not realized until one walks on the exact line where the land meets the sea, experiencing the two forces working together.

The beach is like no other environment on earth. It is a barren desert devoid of vegetation yet repleat with life. It is exposed to blistering sun and incessant ocean breezes, awaiting the embrace of the sea twice each day. And, twice each day, it is released from that embrace and returns to its separate identity. This is misleading, because the water, waves and wind work together with the sand to keep the beach a smoothly functioning environment in dynamic equilibrium.

Nothing should live in an environment like the beach, yet a million things do. Some creatures venture from the land to this edge, stay a while and leave: raccoons who pry open shells, pelicans who feed from the surf, shorebirds who probe for mollusks, and even alligators, who sometimes float in the waves. Some animals venture from the ocean depths, stay a while and return to the sea: the sea turtles, most notably, or horseshoe crabs. Sand dollars, starfish and jellyfish, victims to the whim of the waves, spend part of their lives at sea and are often found dead on the shore. And some creatures live on the water's edge year round; entire colonies of sea creatures surviving in harmony with the wind, sun and salt immersions, as if they couldn't wish for a more comfortable home.

Crabs make their home in this interface. Conchs, whelks and coquinas, cockleshells, olive shells and moonsnails burrow beneath the wet sand and feed on microscopic organisms, all the time trying to keep themselves from being eaten.

Loggerhead sea turtles need this environment to survive. One of South Carolina's endangered species, they come ashore from April to October, laying an average of 126 eggs. Loggerhead nestings have dropped drastically in this state since the 1950s and 1960s. The reasons vary. Sea turtles return to where they were born to lay their eggs. But lights from shorefront development confuse them, and they will not lay, returning instead to the ocean. Nor will they lay where man disturbs them. At one time sea turtle eggs were gathered as delicacies. Today that is illegal. But raccoons and other predators steal the eggs, and sea birds pick off the newborn as they scramble to the ocean. Adult turtles are drowned when caught in the giant nets of offshore fishermen. The turtle cannot survive alongside man unless extreme precautions are taken: for example, reducing and altering the lighting along the beach as was done successfully at Kiawah Island, and monitoring nesting sites to keep predators away. Federal legislation requires fishermen to use "turtle excluder devices," or TEDs, in their nets, but it is not known if that will be enough to keep the turtles from extinction.

Just above the coastal edge, where the waves don't reach, a different environment exists. Here, the dune systems form, with plants using specilized adaptation to survive. The frail-looking sea oat is a master at this. It takes root miraculously on flat, windswept beaches. With its first, tentative leaf cluster, it forms the smallest of windbreaks. This tiny respite allows a little sand to build up behind the first leaf. This, in turn, affords the sea oat more soil so it grows bigger and forms a better windbreak. A dune is forming. Joining the sea oat are shrubby sea elder and sea kale. Eventually, a colony of hardy plants anchors on and just behind the dunes. From this cycle, entire dune systems form — some as mammoth as the quarter-mile high dunes of North Carolina's Outer Banks. To observe the sea oats, dancing in the golden October sunsets, one would not imagine that this graceful plant actually keeps the dunes in place.

On the back side of the dunes colorful orange and black gaillardia thrives; so does pale and delicate evening primrose, opening its yellow blossoms toward evening. Many of the plants — sandspurs, prickly pear cactus and beargrass, for example — sport prickly leaves or spiny stems to ward off plant-eating animals and to keep harmful sand and salt off them. Low growing plants like pennywort and vines like morning glory and smilax grow abundantly on the dunes, adapting to the constant wind by keeping low to the ground. Another method of adaptation is the thick, fleshy stems and branches of plants such as sea kale, which help retain moisture in the arid environment.

The dunes and sandspits offshore, despite their seeming barrenness, are critical habitat for wildlife. Several species of shore birds, the Wilson's plover and oystercatcher, for instance, nest in dunes. Black skimmers, gulls, and terns use the sand islands as their breeding and nursery grounds. So do brown pelicans, once endangered due to ingestion of pesticides, but making a strong comeback in the Lowcountry. Important rookeries exist at Bird Key in the Stono River and Marsh Island at Cape Romain.

The dunes form the first system of defense against hurricanes and Northeasters. Without the dunes, the sea would rage over the island and marshes toward the mainlaind. More precisely, the dunes redistribute the sand, wind and water, allowing just so much through and over. The threat of hurricanes here is a deadly serious one, and the integrity of the shore, dune system and barrier island is critical to the

defense against hurricane-force winds and waves. Written reports tell of hurricanes hitting the South Carolina coast in 1700, 1713, 1728, 1752, 1804. Official reports start in 1878. Since then, 30 hurricanes have come ashore on this coast at an average of one every four or five years. Some caused extensive damage and loss of life; others grazed the land, leaving erosional damage and flooding. There have been times when hurricanes hit three years in a row, or twice in one year. At other times, more than a decade elapsed between landfalls. At the time of this writing, it has been 28 years since the last hurricane did serious damage to the Lowcountry — Gracie in September of 1959 and before that, Hazel in 1954. Today, old timers who have seen bad hurricanes, and historians who study the records, know that a hurricane on these shores is inevitable, and long overdue. And while hurricanes evoke fear, they do have an important function — their heavy rains replenish underground aquifers.

It has only been in recent times that knowledge of coastal ecology has brought us to understand the many complex and interrelated functions of the seaside environment. The sea oat is critical to the life of the dunes, the dunes are critical to the life of the barriers, and the barriers are critical to the land masses behind them. Similarly, we have learned that the marshes, considered at one time worthless unless they could be filled for development, are vital to the survival of millions of marine and other creatures.

The coastal areas are in dire straits today. Poorly understood functions that have kept the islands alive and thriving for thousands of years have been tampered with almost beyond repair. The main culprit is development on shifting sands, and subsequent efforts to stop the shifting sand. Erosion is one of the most hotly discussed topics in the Lowcountry today. On the beaches of Bulls, Capers and Dewees islands, severe erosion has cut into maritime forests, leaving the "bones" of dead trees well into the surf and creating one of the most arresting scenes anywhere in the Lowcountry. Yet the erosion hurts nothing and nature continues to perform as it must. It is only on developed barriers such as Isle of Palms and Seabrook Island that erosion is seen as destructive. The "threat" is only to beach houses that were built precariously close to the shore in the first place.

The ultimate truth of the Lowcountry, shaped and moulded by nature and altered over centuries by man, is that it is still a hauntingly beautiful landscape. Despite man, or because of man? It is hard to say. Man and nature have come to tenuous terms here. Today, there are men and women who work to protect the environment. The job, they have come to see, is never ending. For each person who wants to sit quietly on a sand dune and watch the sun rise on a peaceful coast, there are ten who want to build condominiums, a dock, a pool and a restaurant. There has to be a balance or the beauty that is here today will surely be lost.

Royal terns, Bird Key, mouth of the Stono River

Eroded oaks in the surf, predawn, Capers Island Preserve

Moon over sea oats and dunes, Hunting Island State Park

Loggerhead turtle returning to sea at dawn, Kiawah Island

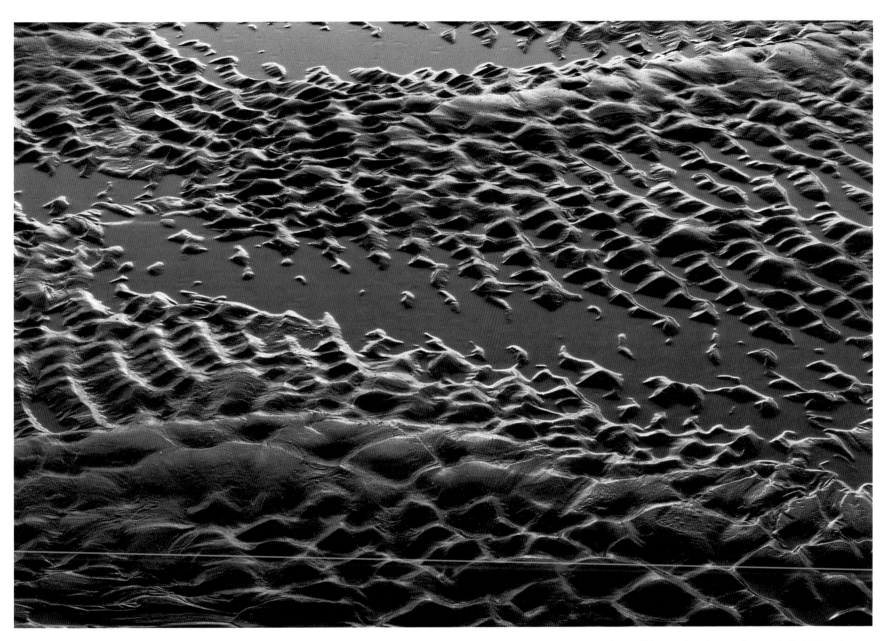

Low-tide sand patterns at sunset, Folly Beach

Winter sky, low tide on the front beach, Capers Island Preserve

Pelican nesting colony, Deveaux Bank, mouth of the North Edisto River

Camphorweed and sea oats, North Island, Yawkey Wildlife Center

Oak tree, surf and full moon, Capers Island Preserve

Palmettos and oak on front beach, Capers Island Preserve

Pen shell, Folly Beach

Surf fisherman, Pawleys Island

COMMENTS ON PHOTOGRAPHY

Nature is made up of living species and objects in a specific habitat. These life forms are interdependent, biologically intertwined; their very survival depends on it. To photograph nature, for me, is to extend this ecological understanding toward an aesthetic consciousness. My senses and intellect become involved in a process I call "visual ecology," wherein I do not see the natural world as consisting of separate objects but, instead, as defined by purely visual relationships. More importantly, these relationships are determined by their context, spontaneous and unique to the moment, and ultimately defined by light and perspective.

This principle of visual ecology dictates my emotional perception of nature by revealing its expressive content. The creative act involves a degree of luck in being at the right place at the right light and having the intuitive sensibilities to recognize and compose the dynamic elements of color, texture, pattern, motion and form.

Without this emotional connection to an object or scene, it is meaningless. For me, the direct, sensual experiencing of nature is paramount. All else is secondary. The photographic process becomes the challenge of translating my emotions to meaningful visual expression. Fundamental to this approach is my belief that nature embodies a spiritual quality and spontaneous vitality. Its creative realization is attained only through total commitment, involving energy, curiosity, patience, persistence, discovery, and finally perfection. The resulting photograph is the consummation of one's passion for the ecological aesthetic.

Photography as an artistic endeavor is often described as a "lonely profession." It is not. Rather, it is a solitary pursuit, sometimes one of long days in remote places, often under unpleasant conditions. But to seek the expressive essence of nature, to experience its character, is for me an addictive freedom, a visual meditation dissolving my sense of self. Photographing the Lowcountry, I am able to transcend my all-too-human fear of isolation, for to love the land is never to be alone. I also carry with me a kindred spirit and respect for other photographers, among them Ernst Haas, Philip Hyde, Eliot Porter, Bill Ratcliffe, and Freeman Patterson. Ultimately, though, I attribute my vision to my family, all painters and interpreters of the natural world.

The majority of photographs in this book were taken over a two to three year period, but some go back ten years, when I first started to explore the Lowcountry. I use two camera systems: Nikon, in 35mm, and a Mamiya RZ, in 6x7 format. When weight and speed of execution are a factor and when photographing wildlife, my Nikon system has been infallible. For more studied landscapes and nature detail the superb quality of the Mamiya is preferable. I have two Nikon F3s with one motor drive. My favorite lenses are the following Nikkors: 28mm f2.8, 50mm f2, 105mm f2.8 macro, 180mm f2.8 ED, 300mm f4.5 ED-IF, 400mm f5.6 ED-IF. With the Mamiya RZ (AE prism) I use a 50mm f4.5, 127mm f3.8, 180mm f4.5, and a 360mm f6. I consider a tripod indispensable and have had many over the years but find the Master Benbo from England (Spiratone) to be without peer.

For film I prefer Kodachrome 25, Kodachrome 64, and Fujichrome 100 in 35mm and Fujichrome 50 for medium format. I often use polarizing and slight warming filters, as well as protective skylight filters. I meter through the camera and rarely record exposure data unless the circumstances are unusual. None of the photographs in this book have been manipulated except for the use of a strobe on pages 93 and 94.

Several other items are worth mentioning. I am in favor of anything that will help relieve the physical burden of camera gear and also facilitate the technical aspects of image making. In this regard, I use a good tripod quick-release for my camera bodies. Several years ago I found that I had twice the stamina and fewer aches by switching from shoulder bags to hip packs. All my lenses and 35mm bodies now ride in Lowe Pro belt packs, which are excellent. I carry film and accessories in a multi-pocket vest, along with my Leitz 10x22 binoculars, which I treasure. Lastly, I would be negligent were I not to mention "Big Red," my VW camper, and "Scoot," my 13-foot Boston Whaler. They help make those long field trips safe, comfortable, and fun.

Prints from the Photographs:

Limited Edition exhibit prints of the photographs in *Lowcountry* may be purchased. Each one is signed and printed personally by the photographer on 16"x20" archival Cibachrome material. Please direct inquiries to: Thomas Blagden, Jr., 44 Society Street, Charleston, SC 29401.

ACKNOWLEDGEMENTS

Lowcountry: The Natural Landscape started as a dream in 1979. A few years ago, however, it fast became a tangible objective. That was due to the insight of one person: Jane Iseley of Legacy Publications. Her enthusiasm and energy were evident from the beginning and never waned throughout the course of the project. I am ever grateful for the editorial and creative freedom she granted me in every aspect of the production of *Lowcountry*. Yet she was always there when needed with a wealth of expertise. As a fine photographer with many books to her own credit, Jane Iseley was especially sensitive to my ideas and problems. Since her initial, almost spontaneous, "Let's do it!," she has let me run with the book. My dream became Jane Iseley's dream.

A very special thanks goes to writers Jane Lareau and Richard Porcher: To Jane for her tireless research and efforts to mold the text to accommodate my photographs...and to Richard, a "walking encyclopedia" on the biology and history of the Lowcountry, for his field knowledge, expertise, and guidance. The chemistry was right and we made a good team.

My sincere thanks to Lee Helmer, who has been a loyal supporter of my work, for applying his considerable talents to designing a book of taste and visual literacy...and for tolerating my looking over his shoulder the whole time.

It is difficult, if not impossible, to succeed in an extended project without a foundation of care and support. I had the best in my wife, Lynn. I am indebted to her for her constant encouragement... for her fine editorial eye... for her company and patience in the field... for her tolerance of all the days and nights when I was gone...and for creating a home to which I always long to return.

The editorial process, both written and visual, is an arduous one at best. In addition to Jane Iseley, Lee Helmer, and Lynn Blagden, many people helped us resolve those "impossible" decisions and contributed significantly toward the success of *Lowcountry*. For their discerning eye toward the photographs I extend my gratitude to John Meffert, Pete Wyrick, Terry Richardson, David Soliday, Luke Platt, West Fraser, my father and mother, and my brother, Allen. For the text I am grateful to Debra Bost, who edited all the writing in this book, and to Ted Rosengarten, author of *Tombee*, who volunteered to review the manuscript and whose comments and knowledge proved invaluable. In addition, I thank Pat and Emmet Robinson, Jane Lareau, and John Meffert for their work on my own writings.

An additional thanks to Pat Kelley and Mike Hale at Kelley's Photo, Mt. Pleasant, South Carolina, for producing the 100-plus working prints from which we assembled the layout and design.

Creating these photographs may seem like a solitary quest, but many of the images in this book were obtained only through the assistance and generosity of others. These are their photographs, too. Among the field biologists I especially want to thank are Phil Wilkinson, who knows the Lowcountry intimately with both an artist's as well as a scientist's sensibilities; Will Post, Curator of Ornithology at the Charleston Museum, for making possible the feather studies and sharing his favorite bird locations; Tom and Sally Murphy, who helped me get the bobcat photograph; Joe Pinson for his consultation and access to Cartwheel Bay; and a special thanks to Keith Bildstein and Jim Johnston, who allowed me to accompany them during their research on Pumpkinseed Island, where I obtained many of my best wading bird photographs. Others who have helped immensely are Ben Moise, a true marshman who introduced me to the barrier islands; Bob Hooper, a devout paddler who was my river consultant; and "Buzz" Botts, whose guidance and knowledge of sea turtles resulted in the loggerhead photograph.

I feel very privileged to have had access to and special assistance at many outstanding locations. To these people and places I extend my sincere appreciation: Ken Williams on the Santee Delta; Tommy Strange, Bill Mace and the staff at Santee Coastal Reserve; Bob Joyner at Yawkey Wildlife Center; George Garris and Donny Browning at Cape Romain National Wildlife Refuge; Ray "Boogie" Tudor at St. Phillips Island; Ann Starck at Deveaux Bank; Norman Brunswig at Beidler Forest/Four Hole Swamp; Middleton Place Foundation; Brookgreen Gardens; and especially the many plantation owners and managers who have generously shared their property and time with me.

Upon examining the photographs in this volume, I realize that many were taken in the company of other photographers. To these friends I give my thanks for their companionship and contagious enthusiasm for the natural world: David Soliday, Luke Platt, Terry Richardson, Phil Wilkinson, and John Meffert. They helped to keep me going. Finally, my deep appreciation goes to my parents, Tom and Martha Blagden, for their irrepressible support and confidence in my endeavors, and to John Henry Dick, much of whose life as an artist-naturalist has been dedicated to the Lowcountry, for sharing with me his friendship and inspiration.

I would also like to acknowledge Nikon and Mamiya camera systems and Kodak and Fuji films for their commitment to quality and perfection in photography.

Thomas Blagden, Jr.

We would like to extend a special thanks to two people who helped make the execution of this book easier. They are Ted Rosengarten, whose extraordinary editing effort, offered as a friend, contributed to the overall excellence of the text, and Marc Hunt, whose contributions and support made the endeavor immeasurably easier. We thank them both.

Jane Lareau & Richard Porcher